MW01639805

ISBN: 9781290614009

Published by:
HardPress Publishing
8345 NW 66TH ST #2561
MIAMI FL 33166-2626

Email: info@hardpress.net
Web: http://www.hardpress.net

St. Rita

levotions to St. Rita

A COMPENDIUM LIFE OF ST. RITA

DEVOTIONAL EXERCISES
NOVENA AND TRIDUUM
INSTRUCTIONS ON NOVENAS ETC.

COMPILED BY
AUGUSTINIAN FATHERS

(English, German, French, Italian and Polish Edition)

PUBLISHED BY
. B. Hansen & Sons, Chicago, Ill.
IMPORTERS & PUBLISHERS

PERMISSU SUPERIORUM:

MARTIN J. GERAGHTY, D. D., O. S. A.
Provincialis Ordinis Sancti Augustini

NIHIL OBSTAT:

J. F. GREEN S. T. B., O. S. A.
Censor Deputatus

IMPRIMATUR:

JACOBUS E. QUIGLEY
Archiepiscopus Chicagiensis

DEVOTIONS IN HONOR OF ST. RITA OF CASCIA, O. S. A.

O BLESSED St. Rita, our patroness and guide, we lay this chaplet at thy feet, a litany, as we do the thoughts, the labors, the sufferings of our lives, that holding daily before our eyes the gentle purity, patience and sanctity of thy example our lives may be lived in some poor image of thine own, even unto life everlasting.

LITANY OF ST. RITA OF CASCIA

Lord, have mercy on us.
Christ, have mercy on us.
Lord, have mercy on us.
Christ, hear us.
Christ, graciously hear us.
God, the Father Almighty, *have mercy on us.*
God, the Son, Redeemer of the world, who hast said: "Ask, and you shall receive; seek, and you shall find; knock, and it shall be opened unto you," *have mercy etc.*

God, the Holy Ghost, Spirit of Wisdom, Understanding, Counsel and Knowledge,

Holy Trinity, one God, Power Infinite,
Holy Mary, who hast never refused those who implored thee, *Pray for us.*

Immaculate Mary, Queen of Heavcn and Earth, *Pray etc.*

Our Lady of the Sacred Heart,
Holy Angels, spirits of humility,
Holy Principalities, charged with the care of religious communities,

Holy Virtues, angels of energy,
Holy Cherubim, angels of light,
St. Rita, advocate of the impossible,
St. Rita, enamored of humility,
St. Rita, consecrated to God,
St. Rita, lover of Jesus crucified,
St. Rita, spouse of Jesus suffering,
St. Rita, penetrated with compassion for our Lord,

St. Rita, crowned by an angel with the sacred crown of thorns,

St. Rita, who didst bear the wound of this supernatural coronation upon thy forehead,

St. Rita, trusting in the tender mercy of Jesus,

St. Rita, importuning our dying Lord with irresistible fervor,

St. Rita, never doubting the answer to prayer,

That we may renounce all self-love, *Pray for us, St. Rita.*

That we may confide in the promises of Christ, *Pray for us, etc.*

That the enemies of our salvation may be put to confusion,

That we may accomplish most perfectly the holy will of God,

That the power of evil over us may be destroyed,

That faith may spread in all its purity over our land,

That a holy zeal may take possession of our hearts,

That we may inspire all with whom we associate with a love for holy purity,

That we may cultivate a delicate charity in all our actions,

That we may be delivered from all avarice, vainglory, or rash judgment,

That great saints may arise in our nation, to edify the people and enlighten the darkness of infidelity,

That we may be delivered from all interior foes,

Lamb of God, who takest away the sins of the world, *spare us, O Lord!*

Lamb of God, who takest away the sins of the world, *graciously hear us, O Lord!*

Lamb of God, who takest away the sins of the world, *have mercy on us, O Lord!*

℣. Pray for us, St. Rita,

℟. That we may be made worthy of the promises of Christ.

LET US PRAY

O God, who in Thine infinite tenderness hast vouchsafed to regard the prayer of Thy servant, Blessed Rita, and dost grant to her supplication that which is impossible to human foresight, skill and efforts, in reward of her compassionate love and firm reliance upon Thy promises; have pity upon our adversity and succor us in our calamities, that the unbeliever may know Thou art the recompense of the humble, the defense of the helpless, and the strength of those who trust in Thee. Through Jesus Christ, our Lord. Amen.

PRAYER TO ST. RITA

O holy protectress of those who are in utmost need, who shinest as a star of hope in the midst of darkness, glorious and blessed St. Rita, bright mirror of the Catholic Church, in patience and fortitude as the patriarch Job, scourge of devils, health of the sick, deliverer of those in extreme need, admiration of Saints, and model of all states; with my whole heart and soul prostrated before and firmly united to the adorable will of my God, through the merits of my only Lord and Saviour, Jesus Christ, and in particular through the merits of His patient wearing of that torturing crown of thorns, which thou, with a tender devotion, didst daily contemplate; through the merits of the most sweet Virgin Mary and thine own excellent graces and virtues, I implore thee to obtain my earnest petition—provided it be for the greater glory of God and my own sanctification (here mention your request), and herein do thou guide and purify my intention, O holy protectress and most dear advocate, so that I may obtain the pardon of all my sins and grace to persevere daily, as thou didst, in walking with courage and generosity and unwavering fidelity through the heavenward path in which the love of my sweet Lord desires to lead me. Amen.

INVOCATIONS TO ST. RITA

St. Rita, Advocate of the Hopeless, pray for us.

St. Rita, Advocate of the Impossible, pray for us.

Three Our Fathers, Hail Marys, Glory be to the Father, etc.

Blessed be God, the Father of our Lord Jesus Christ, Father of Mercy and God of all Consolation, who, through the intercession of St. Rita, comforts us in all our tribulations. Amen.

(A decree, August 11, 1906, grants an indulgence of 300 days to all who once a day devoutly recite the following prayer in honor of St. Rita of Cascia.)

O glorious St. Rita, who didst miraculously participate in the sorrowful Passion of our Lord Jesus Christ, obtain for me the grace to suffer with resignation the troubles of this life, and protect me in all my needs. Amen.

PRAYER

Holy Patroness of those in need, St. Rita, so humble, pure and patient, whose pleadings with your Divine Spouse are irresistible, obtain for us from your crucified Jesus our request. Be propitious toward us for the greater glory of God and yourself, and we promise to honor and sing your praises ever after. Amen.

PRAYER TO ST. RITA

O glorious St. Rita, perfect disciple of the meek and humble Nazarene, because of that most profound humility which thou didst exercise amidst the lowliest duties of the convent, after being introduced by thy holy Protector into the sacred cloister of Cascia through closed doors, where following the Rule of St. Augustine, thou didst lead a life hidden with Christ in God, we pray thee obtain for us from that God who resisteth the proud and imparteth His gifts to the humble, the grace to conquer the passion of pride within us, that noxious root of all our woes, so we may become worthy to be raised up to the eternal glory of Heaven in imitation of our Divine Redeemer, while we honor Him.

Our Father, Hail Mary, Glory, etc.

THE ADVOCATE OF THE HOPELESS

(St. Rita was canonized May 24, 1900. She is universally called "The Saint of Impossible Things," as her intercession has been found available in the most desperate cases.)

HYMN TO ST. RITA OF CASCIA*

Chorus:

Come, virgins chaste, pure brides, draw near:
Let each exult and Heaven hear
The hymn which grateful accents raise,
Our song of joy in Rita's praise.

By fast her sinless frame is weak;
Her livid flesh the scourges streak.
In pity for her Savior's woes,
Her days and even nights are closed.

The thorn-wound on her brow is shown,
The crimson rose in winter blown,
And full-ripe figs in frozen tree
At Rita's wish the wonders see.

*This hymn is the translation of the hymn of Lauds, office of St. Rita, approved by Decret. S. R. C., Nov. 24, 1900.

The widowed spouse and wedded wife
The way to Heaven see in her life;
The way secure our Rita trod,
In life's dim day, through pain to God.

Praise to the Father and the Son,
Praise to the Spirit, Three in One;
O grant us grace in Heaven to reign
Through Rita's prayer and lifelong pain.

℣. Thou hast signed Thy servant Rita

℟. With the signs of Thy Love and Passion.

LET US PRAY

O God, who didst deign to confer on St. Rita, for imitating Thee in love of her enemies, the favor of bearing in her heart and brow the marks of Thy Love and Passion, grant, we beseech Thee, that through her intercession and merit, we may, pierced by the thorns of compunction, ever contemplate the sufferings of Thy Passion, who liveth and reigneth forever and ever. Amen.

Three Our Fathers, Hail Marys, Glory be to the Father, etc.

OCCASIONAL PRAYERS IN HONOR OF ST. RITA

MEMORARE IN HONOR OF ST. RITA

Remember, O holy protectress of those in extreme need, that no one ever turned to thee in affliction, besought thy assistance, or implored thy intercession and was left unaided. With a firm reliance upon thy favor at the Throne of Grace, I, a suppliant, come to thee, Blessed Rita, bright Saint of the Impossible! Hearken thou to my petitions. Amen.

PRAYER TO KNOW ONE'S VOCATION

O glorious St. Rita, to whose guiding care I have committed myself, in this the most serious affair of my life; come to my assistance. Obtain for me, from the crucified Savior, the grace to walk only in that way which He has decreed shall be the means to the end for which I was created, the enjoyment of God in heaven. Amen.

PRAYER TO BE SAID IN ANY NECESSITY

O holy Rita, upon whom God did confer such singular favors during thy stay on this earth; pray for me and obtain the grace, first to know and detest my sins, and to increase in virtue; and particularly that I may be freed from my present affliction (here mention request), provided such liberation be not contrary to the Divine Will nor detrimental to my salvation. In this desire and in all other things I commit and subject myself to the Disposition and Will of the Most High God, and to thy maternal judgment, O holy Rita. Amen.

TRIDUUM IN HONOR OF ST. RITA

(For Private Devotion)

(The following prayers may be used as a triduum in honor of St. Rita, to be said either on three consecutive days or on three consecutive Thursdays. An omisison of one day breaks the triduum.)

First Day

ROSARY OF THE BLESSED VIRGIN

PRAYER

DIRECT, we beseech Thee, O Lord, all our actions by Thy holy inspirations, and carry them on by Thy gracious assistance, that every prayer and other good work of ours may begin always from Thee, and by Thee be happily ended: through Christ our Lord. Amen.

O blessed Rita, I take thee this day for my special protectress and advocate with God. In all humility I rejoice with thee, because thou wast chosen of God for the special marks of His favors. Obtain for me, by thy prayers, a spirit of true courage in all the trials of this life. Make it thy special care, O blessed advocate, to obtain for me an efficacious love of God, a strong love, a pure love, enabling me to surmount all difficulties which might hinder my union with God in life, so that I may become one with Him forever after death.

O glorified Rita, look down upon me still exiled and send me hope and consolation. Obtain for me the grace of imitating thy virtues: and if it be God's Holy Will, I would beg of thee to add thy prayers to mine for the obtaining of this, my special request (mention it).

(A decree of August 11, 1906, grants an indulgence of 300 days to all who once a day devoutly recite the following prayer in honor of St. Rita of Cascia.)

O glorious St. Rita, who didst miraculously participate in the sorrowful Passion of our Lord Jesus Christ, obtain for me the grace to suffer with resignation the troubles of this life, and protect me in all my needs. Amen.

Three Our Fathers, Hail Marys, Glory be to the Father, etc.

Second Day

ROSARY OF THE BLESSED VIRGIN

PRAYER

Direct, we beseech Thee, etc. (as on first day).

O glorious Rita, thou who, while on earth, wast a mirror of innocence and a model of penance; O saintly heroine, specially chosen by God to wear on thy heart and brow the marks of His love and Passion, look down from Heaven graciously upon my soul and hear my prayers. Obtain for me such a love for Jesus suffering, that ever meditating on His Passion I may make His suffering mine; that I may draw from the wounds of my Savior, as from so many founts of salvation, the grace of lamenting my sins and a firm will to imitate thee in penance, if I have not followed thee in innocence.

O glorified Rita, look down upon me still exiled and send me hope and consolation. Obtain for me the grace of imitating thy virtues; and if it be God's Holy Will, I would beg of thee to add thy prayers to mine for the obtain for me the grace to suffer with (mention it).

(A decree of August 11, 1906, grants an indulgence of 300 days to all who once a day devoutly recite the following prayer in honor of St. Rita of Cascia.)

O glorious St. Rita, who didst miraculously participate in the sorrowful Passion of our Lord Jesus Christ, obtaining of this my special request resignation the troubles of this life, and protect me in all my needs. Amen.

Three Our Fathers, Hail Marys, Glory be to the Father, etc.

Third Day

ROSARY OF THE BLESSED VIRGIN

PRAYER

Direct, we beseech Thee, etc. (as on first day).

O happy Rita, who hast already crossed over the sea of our mortality, be solicitous for me in my manifold misery. Reach forth thy hands to me, O advocate of desperate cases, and guide my tottering footsteps, that gaining strength through thy aid I may walk more confidently in the by-paths of the Saviour. Obtain for me faith and perseverance, that I may serve God in fear and so keep His Commandments. I beseech thee, O holy Rita, to send me from thy home in Heaven a few drops of the wine of thy charity, for my soul is dry with the dryness of the world and its pleasures. Come to me, a miserable sinner, and loose the bonds of my captivity. Take me apart from the world-maddened crowds that I may sit with thee and God Almighty; that I may hear the voice of my God breaking in silence to my aching heart.

O glorified Rita, look down upon me still exiled and send me hope and consolation. Obtain for me the grace of imitating thy virtues and if it be God's Holy Will, I would beg of thee to add thy prayers to mine for the obtaining of this special request (mention it).

(A decree of August 11, 1906, grants an indulgence of 300 days to all who once a day devoutly recite the following prayer in honor of St. Rita of Cascia.)

O glorious St. Rita, who didst miraculously participate in the sorrowful Passion of our Lord Jesus Christ, obtain for me the grace to suffer with resignation the troubles of this life, and protect me in all my needs. Amen.

Three Our Fathers, Hail Marys, Glory be to the Father, etc.

NOVENA IN HONOR OF ST. RITA

(For Private Devotion)

(The following prayers may be used as a novena in honor of Saint Rita to be said either on nine consecutive days, or on nine consecutive Thursdays. An omission of one day breaks the novena.)

First Day

FROM her childhood, St. Rita had received a wonderful gift of prayer. This gift she developed in a striking manner during the years of her early youth. Whoever wished to see her was certain of finding her either at home or in the parish church, which was her favorite place of prayer, where she spent entire hours in meditation and devotion to the great edification of all. This practice she continued during her whole life as a wife and mother, but especially after her miraculous entrance into the religious state. As a nun her prayers were offered in the darkness of the night, in the early morning and throughout the day; in one word, prayer was her life, for not even for one moment could she withdraw herself from the presence of her Uncreated Love.

Let prayer, then, be the subject of your thoughts on the first day of your novena. Frequently recite some little ejaculation during the day and ask our Divine Lord in union with the Apostles to teach you how to pray and to fill your heart with the spirit of prayer.

EXERCISES

Say the Rosary of the Blessed Virgin, the Litany of St. Rita, page 5, and the following prayer:

O blessed Rita, wonderful model of prayer for those in every state and condition of life, pray to your Divine Spouse, with whom your intercession is so powerful and your prayers so efficacious, that the spirit of prayer may descend into my heart and ever remain there. Obtain for me also, beloved patron, that like you I may find my chief delight in having recourse to my divine Master; that like you I may be worthy to be numbered amongst His chosen disciples; that He may protect me during life from the enemies of my soul's salvation and from every danger, and at the moment of my death place me among the heavenly multitude of the blessed. Amen.

Then say the prayer, "O holy Protectress," page 9.

Three Our Fathers, Hail Marys, Glory be to the Father, etc.

Second Day

The foundation of every virtue is humility. God resists the proud and gives His grace to the humble. Where pride reigns there can be no virtue. That Rita is the great Saint she is today is due mainly to the fact of her humility. She practised this virtue as a child when she never tried or wished even to prefer herself to anyone. As the wife of a cruel husband she maintained a profound humility. Her models were Christ Himself, who told His disciples and followers to learn to be meek and humble of heart, Mary the Mother of God, who notwithstanding that she alone of all the daughters of Eve was selected to be the Mother of the God-Man, cried out: "Behold the handmaid of the Lord," and St. John the Baptist, of whom Christ gave the testimony that he was the greatest born of woman, who declared himself to be but the "voice of one crying in the wilderness." In the convent she practised this virtue to an heroic degree, always taking the lowest place, performing the most menial duties, and shunning any work that would in any way bring her into prominence.

In imitation of St. Rita, then, be humble, love to be despised, and do not repine because the world does not treat you as you think you deserve to be treated. Frequently today repeat the ejaculation, "Jesus meek and humble of heart, make my heart like unto Thine."

EXERCISES

Rosary of the Blessed Virgin, Litany of St. Rita, page 5, and the following prayer:

O glorious St. Rita, perfect disciple of the meek and humble Nazarene, because of that most profound humility which thou didst exercise amidst the lowliest duties of the convent after being introduced by thy holy Protector into the sacred cloister of Cascia through closed doors, where, following the rule of St. Augustine, thou didst lead a life hidden with Christ in God, we pray thee obtain for us from that God who resisteth the proud and imparteth His gifts to the humble, the grace to conquer the passion of pride within us, that noxious root of all our woes, so we may become worthy to be raised up to the eternal glory of heaven in imitation of our Divine Redeemer. Amen.

Then say the prayer, "O holy Protectress," page 9.

Three Our Fathers, Hail Marys, Glory be to the Father, etc.

Third Day

The Saints were men and women just the same as those now living. They had the same passions, the same temptations as we have. We have the same means and remedies to overcome the great enemies of our salvation, viz., the world, the flesh and the devil, as they had, and yet unfortunately it must be admitted that there is a great difference between the saints and us. The chief cause of this is that the saints guided and directed their actions by the spirit of faith. In everything that happened to them they beheld the hand of God and adored His Holy Will. St. Rita had an intense desire to consecrate her life to God in the religious state, but it was only after long years of patient waiting, years filled with suffering and sorrow, that she was to enjoy the fulfillment of her cherished wish. Yet she was ever cheerful, because she felt that these sufferings were permitted by a loving God and that she could do nothing more meritorious than to submit to His Holy Will.

Let it be our practice during this novena and the remainder of our lives to imitate God's saints and especially our dear St. Rita in bearing patiently all the adversities of life as coming from God for our own welfare and repeat frequently the ejaculation, "Blessed be the Holy Will of God."

EXERCISES

Rosary of the Blessed Virgin, Litany of St. Rita, page 5, and the following prayer:

O glorious St. Rita, chosen friend of Jesus Christ, help me by your intercession and obtain for me the spirit of faith as lively as that which you yourself possessed, that it may guide and direct me in all the adversities of life and teach me to adore in all things the Holy Will of God. May this holy faith lift me above the things of time and show me in accordance with the science of all the saints that I should not place my heart on objects that will so soon pass away, but rather that the only royal road to the kingdom of heaven is the patient endurance of whatever may happen here below. O good Jesus, grant me through the prayers of St. Rita, the spirit of faith, that glorious gift which the prince of the Apostles asked with such fervor: "Lord, increase our faith." May my life be in accordance with the teaching of your holy Gospel and may I be able to say with my dying breath, "I have kept the faith," and now am ready for my eternal reward. Amen.

Then say the prayer, "O holy Protectress," page 9.

Three Our Fathers, Hail Marys, Glory be to the Father, etc.

Fourth Day

If there was one virtue more than another that distinguished itself in the life of St. Rita, it was her obedience. As a child it was in the light of this virtue that she regulated all her actions. She regarded the slightest wish of her parents as a command of God which she could not violate. It was in obedience to their wish that she for the time gave up her ardent desire of becoming a nun and entered a marriage on which her heart was not set. But no sooner did she become a wife than she immediately realized that her duty was to regard her husband as a master to whom that obedience and reverential fear are due which the Church owes to her head, Christ. Though her husband was by nature brutal, and frequently ill-treated her, she obeyed his every wish. It was, however, as a nun that she practised this virtue in an heroic degree. All her actions were so many acts of obedience, or, rather her whole conventual life was an uninterrupted act of the humblest, truest and readiest obedience.

Learn from St. Rita to prize this holy virtue; be faithful in your observance of the laws of God and His holy Church. Look upon your superiors, whoever they may be, as God's representatives, and in doing their will, as long as it is not sinful, you may be sure you are pleasing God, who one day will reward you as He rewarded St. Rita.

EXERCISES

Rosary of the Blessed Virgin, Litany of St. Rita, page 5, and the following prayer:

O glorious St. Rita, bright ornament of the Augustinian Order; model of obedience during your whole life; perfect disciple of Him who came on earth to do the will of His Heavenly Father, and who was obedient in all things even unto the death of the cross; obtain for me by your powerful intercession the grace to render myself perfectly obedient and submissive to all God's designs in my regard. May I obtain also the grace to behold God in the person of my superiors, spiritual and temporal, and thus render them that loyal and loving service which characterized your every act. Amen.

Then say the prayer, "O holy Protectress," page 9.

Three Our Fathers, Hail Marys, Glory be to the Father, etc.

Fifth Day

In her youth, even while yet a child, Rita's only desire was to consecrate herself to God in the religious state. But alas! what trials and sufferings were to come upon her before she was to experience the joy of this religious consecration. In obedience to her parents' wish she entered the married state. Here her life was one cross after another, caused by a wayward husband,

and children who followed in the footsteps of their unruly father. After the death of husband and children, when she tried to gain admittance to the convent, she again, more than once, was refused and finally, when enrolled among the virgins of Cascia, the afflictions sent her by Heaven itself were so great that she was obliged to shut herself off from the sweet companionship of her sisters. Yet in all these trials, great indeed though they were, and lasting during her whole life, she was never known to utter a word of complaint. Rather hers was ever a peaceful and joyous countenance, and on her lips was a word of comfort for every sufferer who came in contact with her. Well did she learn the patience and resignation of her beloved Master.

You too, her devoted client, be sure to imitate these special virtues and you may be certain that as God rewarded St. Rita so too will He bless you. Remember that every pain, no matter how slight, if it be borne with patience, will become a jewel of infinite price in your crown of glory.

EXERCISES

Rosary of the Blessed Virgin, Litany of St. Rita, page 5, and the following prayer:

O blessed Rita, model of patience and resignation to the will of God, in all your trials; how much I need the consolation afforded by meditating on your sufferings, and learning from you never to be downcast but always to raise my eyes to heaven, there seeking, as you did, the strength to bear patiently the various ills of life. Obtain for me from your Divine Spouse and Model those virtues of patience and resignation, the true philosophers' stone which will change the ordinary trials of life into the precious pearls of a glorious diadem, similar to that which now adorns your brow, and which will be forever yours in reward for your patiently bearing the cross your heavenly Father sent you. Amen.

Then say the prayer, "O holy Protectress," page 9.

Three Our Fathers, Hail Marys, Glory be to the Father, etc.

Sixth Day

When St. Rita was yet a child she obtained the consent of her parents to set aside a little room as an oratory. The walls of this room she decorated with pictures of our Lord's Passion, and therein she shut herself, as in the midst of all delights. The constant object of her thoughts during her whole life, and which caused the ecstasies of her soul as well as the most ardent love of her heart, was the Passion of her Crucified Spouse. She felt herself absorbed into the Crucified One for whom alone she lived. It was her pious custom daily to prostrate herself before the crucifix and there to pour out the loving longings of her heart, that all might do homage to the Son of God, who, out of love, suffered such torments for them. One day while thus kneeling in prayer she saw one of the thorns from the crown of the crucifix detach itself and strike her on the left side of the forehead with such force that it almost penetrated the bone, causing her exquisite pain. This wound she carried with her to death.

Dear client of St. Rita, there is no form of meditation simpler or more advantageous than meditation on the sorrowful Passion of Christ. Let it be your chief delight, with St. Rita, in whose honor you are making this Novena, to dwell with loving thoughts on this Sacred Passion, especially today. Think of it during your work, your free time, and ask St. Rita, to obtain for you the same delights from this holy exercise as inundated her pure soul.

EXERCISES

Rosary of the Blessed Virgin, Litany of St. Rita, page 5, and the following prayer:

O sweet Lord Jesus, Who became man for the salvation of the human race, and who suffered such untold pains and humiliations that guilty man might be restored again to the love and friendship of his Creator, grant that through the merits of blessed Rita, the sorrows of Your Passion may be the constant object of my thoughts and aspirations. Imprint deeply in my heart the love of Your Passion, and grant that in imitation of my glorious patron, St.

Rita, I may deserve to hear an answer to my prayers and may come with her to eternal happiness. Amen.

Then say the prayer, "O holy Protectress," page 9.

Three Our Fathers, Hail Marys, Glory be to the Father, etc.

Seventh Day

Forgiveness of injuries is a duty incumbent on every Christian who claims to be a follower of Christ. The necessity of this duty is taught not only by the positive precepts of our divine Lord, but far more forcibly by the example of His life, for when hanging on the cross, His dying words were a prayer to His heavenly Father for the pardon of His murderers. "Father, forgive them for they know not what they do." So thoroughly was St. Rita convinced of the necessity of pardoning her enemies, and so desirous was she of imitating the example of her beloved Spouse that she did not for a moment hesitate to pardon sincerely from her heart the cruel men who brutally murdered her unfortunate husband. She too in imitation of the example of the dying Redeemer offered fervent supplications to the divine mercy for those wicked murderers.

We, the clients of St. Rita, wishing to honor her and obtain her protection during this novena, should bear continually in mind that there is no better way to insure her help than by a fervent and loyal imitation of her virtues.

Resolve, then, today to banish from your heart all ill-will and uncharitable feelings toward those who may have done you any injury. Forgive, and as you deal with others, so will your heavenly Father deal with you, for charity covers a multitude of sins.

EXERCISES

Rosary of the Blessed Virgin, Litany of St. Rita, page 5, and the following prayer:

O dearest Lord, how many times I have offended You and how kind You have been to me in granting me the grace of repentance. I acknowledge that my life has been one of ingratitude for the numberless favors which You bestowed upon me. I thank You especially for the various lessons of virtue You have given me through the life of blessed Rita, and beg of You to impress on my heart the lesson of forgiveness of injuries. O blessed Rita, spouse of Jesus suffering, you who were so cruelly treated by others during life and yet pardoned from your inmost heart the injuries you received, obtain for me the favor to love all men, even those who may do me the greatest injuries. Amen.

Then say the prayer, "O holy Protectress," page 9.

Three Our Fathers, Hail Marys, Glory be to the Father, etc.

Eighth Day

St. Rita, one of the greatest Saints whom God has been pleased to raise up in modern times, may be truly considered a model for every condition in life as well as a bright exemplar of the virtues that ought to adorn every good and fervent Christian. Holy Church has solemnly declared that she practised these virtues in an heroic degree. However, there is one practice that in her holy life stands out more prominently than all the others, and that is her love and devotion toward Jesus in the Holy Eucharist. As a child, she spent her free time in church speaking to the Prisoner of Love on the altar. As a wife and mother, her chief delight was to receive into her loving heart the divine Spouse of her soul. As a nun, she spent whole nights prostrated before the Tabernacle, and when the first rays of dawn began to break on her long vigil, she complained because other duties called her away from those sacred precincts. Yet no matter what duties she was called on to perform, her affections were ever directed to that sacred spot where her treasure was.

Oh, dear client of St. Rita, learn from her that no devotion is of any account that does not bring you into closer contact with the Most Blessed Sacrament. Receive it frequently and worthily and today prepare yourself to receive it worthily tomorrow, the closing day of your novena.

EXERCISES

Rosary of the Blessed Virgin, Litany of St. Rita, page 5, and the following prayer:

O sweet Lord Jesus, who out of love for me dost remain day and night, a Prisoner of Love in the Most Holy Sacrament of the Altar, often lonely and neglected by those You love, but more so by me. O grant me, dear Jesus, through the intercession of Your beloved servant Rita, to find my joy and consolation in visiting You in this Sacrament, and in receiving You into my heart. I desire now to receive You but, alas, I am not prepared. Come then into my soul in spirit. Prepare it for that happy moment tomorrow when I will have the happiness of receiving You sacramentally as the crowning work of this novena, and grant me through the intercession of St. Rita the favors I am asking You during these days of prayer. Amen.

Then say the prayer, "O holy Protectress," page 9.

Three Our Fathers, Hail Marys, Glory be to the Father, etc.

Ninth Day

Coming near the end of her holy and miraculous life, St. Rita felt that she was languishing with love for her heavenly bridegroom. This love was the characteristic of her pure life, the guiding principle of her every act, and now in her last moments on earth it caused her to desire her freedom from the ties of her body so that she might take her flight to enjoy for all eternity her Uncreated Good. Our divine Lord, accompanied by His Most Holy Mother, appeared to her and announced the joyous tidings that in three days she should be taken from this world and all her pains, and be received into Paradise to receive the reward of her virtues and sufferings. With what fervor did she not immediately prepare to receive the last sacraments and fortify herself for that long journey. She received them with a fervor more easily imagined than described, and then, with her eyes turned toward the abode of the blessed, her pure soul took its flight thither where she now lives an immortal life, the reward of her heroic virtues.

Her precious death took place on the night of May 22, 1457, the last day of the week, a day specially consecrated to the honor of the Mother of God, whom, after God Himself, she loved with her whole heart. Be devoted to Mary, and ask her frequently to intercede for you at the hour of your death.

EXERCISES

Rosary of the Blessed Virgin, Litany of St. Rita, page 5, and the following prayer:

O glorious St. Rita, filled with love for your heavenly Father, take me today, unworthy though I be, under your powerful protection, and obtain for me the favor I am seeking during this novena (name your request). I beseech you also to obtain for me the ineffable grace of loving God with my whole heart during the remainder of my life, of loving Him above all things in imitation of the bright example of your life, that thus I may merit as you did to die in the sweet embrace of Jesus and Mary. O teach me, dear Saint, to prepare myself for that moment on which so much depends, and obtain that death may be for me the entrance to eternal life. Amen.

Then say the prayer, "O holy Protectress," page 9.

Three Our Fathers, Hail Marys, Glory be to the Father, etc.

BLESSING OF THE ROSES

(On the feast day, May 22)

Blessing of the Roses for the Sick, on the feast of St. Rita of Cascia, Widow of the Order of St. Augustine.

℣. Adjutorium nostrum in nomine Domini.

℟. Qui fecit coelum, et terram.

℣. Domine exaudi orationem meam.

℟. Et clamor meus ad te veniat.

℣. Dominus vobiscum.

℟. Et cum Spiritu tuo.

Oremus

Deus, creator, et conservator generis humani, dator gratiae spiritualis, et largitor humanae salutis, benedictione sancta tua bene † dic has rosas, quas pro gratiis ex-

℣. Our help is in the name of the Lord.

℟. Who hath made heaven and earth.

℣. O Lord, hear my prayer.

℟. And let my cry come unto Thee.

℣. The Lord be with you.

℟. And with thy Spirit.

Let us pray

O God, Creator and Preserver of the human race, giver of spiritual grace and dispenser of salvation to men, with Thy holy benediction bless these roses which out of de-

solvendis cum devotione et veneratione beatae Ritae, hodie tibi praesentamus, et petimus benedici, et infunde in eis per virtutem sanctae Cru ✠ cis benedictionem; ut quibuscumque infirmitatibus appositae fuerint, seu illorum, qui eas in domibus suis, vel locis cum devotione habuerint, aut portaverint, infirmitates sanentur; discedant diaboli, contremiscant, et fugiant pavidi cum suis ministris de habitationibus illis, nec amplius tibi servientes inquietare praesumant. Per Dominum nostrum, etc.

℟. Amen.

votion and veneration to blessed Rita we present Thee today and in thanksgiving beseech Thee to bless. Infuse into them Thy benediction by the power of the Holy Cross, so that all infirmities, to which they may be applied, whether of those who with devotion preserve them in their homes or other places, or who carry them about with them may be healed. May the devils, put to confusion, and terrified, flee from these habitations and never more dare to disturb those who serve Thee. Through our Lord, etc.

℟. Amen.

(Then the roses are sprinkled with holy water and incensed).

Oremus

Exaudi nos Deus Salutaris noster; ut sicut de beatae Ritae festivitate gaudemus; ita piae devotionis erudiamur affectu. Per Christum Dominum nostrum.

℟. Amen.

Let us pray

Hear us, O merciful God, that as we rejoice in the feast of Blessed Rita so we may be enlightened by the love of pious devotion. Through Christ our Lord.

℟. Amen.

HOW TO MAKE A NOVENA

One of the essential qualities of prayer is perseverance, as is evident from the words of St. James, who says that the continual prayer of a just man availeth much (James V. 16). Our divine Lord gives us in His own example, on the eve of His bitter Passion, a lively proof of perseverance; for the inspired Evangelist says: "He prayed the third time saying the self-same words" (Matt. XXVI. 44). For these reasons Holy Mother Church has approved the practice of praying during certain periods for some favor or blessing which we desire our Father in heaven to bestow upon us.

She has her special times for prayer, such as the holy seasons of Lent and Advent. Besides this, we have *nine days'* devotions commonly called novenas, either in honor of some one of the three Divine Persons, as the novena to the Holy Ghost, or to some of the Saints through whose favor with God we confidently hope to obtain our cherished requests.

A novena, then, consists of certain prayers or devotions continuing uninterruptedly for nine days. These days may be either successive days or they may be one special day each week for nine successive weeks. No special or set forms of prayers are required. In order, however, to help the clients of St. Rita to partake of the wonderful favors she obtains so abundantly for those who make the novena in her honor, the prayers herein set down may be used with much fruit. If a day be missed either in the nine consecutive days or weeks the novena is broken and must be commenced over again.

As the state of grace is one of the surest means of partaking of God's graces and blessings, each person making a novena ought to try as often as possible during the nine weeks to approach the sacraments of Penance and Holy Eucharist, and during the nine days, if the novena be made on consecutive days, these sacraments should be worthily received on or before the last day of the devotions. If it be possible the novena to St. Rita ought to be made at her shrine, though it may be made privately at home.

Faith in God's promises, hope in His goodness, and resignation to His Divine Will, joined to purity of heart and perseverance are the conditions of fruitful prayer, the prayer of which Christ spoke when he said: "Amen, amen, I say to you, if you ask the Father anything in my name He will give it to you."

SAINT RITA OF CASCIA

UMBRIA, an important province of Italy, is distinguished in the annals of the Church as the land of saints and scholars. Three great religious institutes reverence it as the birthplace of their respective founders, St. Benedict, St. Francis of Assisi, and St. Clare—proud claims that entitle Umbria to the gratitude of all Christendom. Not less generous has she been to the Augustinians, upon whose calendar we find no less than eight servants of God honored with Mass and Office, whose birth was likewise in this same portion of Italy. Among these is numbered St. Clare of Montefalco, recently honored with the title of Saint, and also Rita of Cascia, of whose eventful life a sketch is here appended, and whose canonization is now a matter of history, having taken place on the 24th of May, 1900.

In the Duchy of Spoleto, amid the hills skirting the Appenines, is situated the ancient town of Cascia, the capital, in former times, of an independent State. The inhabitants of this mountainous district were thrifty people, imbued with deep sentiments of love and loyalty toward their holy religion. During the turbulent days of the 15th century, when the rival powers of France and Spain were contesting for the mastery of Italy, Cascia maintained an unswerving devotion to the Sovereign Pontiffs, whose territory it had become by the free choice of its inhabitants.

During the latter part of the fourteenth century, Rocca Porrena, a hamlet not more than a mile from Cascia, was the home of an aged couple, Antonio Mancini and Amata Ferri. During their wedded life they had become endeared to the townsfolk, not less for the sanctity of their lives than for their unselfish devotion to all in distress. Though not rich in this world's wealth, they found manifold opportunities of befriending the needy and of exercising a far-reaching influence for good among their neighbors and acquaintances. The mission of peacemakers among the inhabitants of Rocca Porrena seemed the special calling of this aged couple. In those days of strife and discord, when arms were too often the sole badge of authority and war the arbiter of rival claims, these athletes of charity loved to appeal to the meekness of Jesus Christ, as the best means to overcome the spirit of discord so rife around them.

In many towns of Umbria there is still preserved the laudable custom of designating each year, by popular consent, some man and woman enjoying universal confidence to act as arbiters in all questions of dispute, and to adjust amicably matters that have set families and homes at variance. For a task so commendable and so befitting the guardian angel of peace, the venerable Antonio and his wife were chosen. Far and familiarly were they known as "The Lord's Peacemakers." And the ready cheerfulness with which their judgments were obeyed was the highest tribute to the intelligence and integrity of this holy couple. But there was one blessing wanting, the possession of which could alone complete the measure of their earthly felicity. God had not deigned to bless the union of Antonio and Amata with offspring, which loss they deplored the more keenly as advancing years seemed to render their desires hopeless and their home more cheerless. Many and heartfelt were the supplications which they conjointly sent up to the Throne of Grace, beseeching this favor of the Most High.

The Lord was witness of the deeds, and He heard the prayers of His just servants, the Mancinis, who in old age were singularly rewarded with the fruition of their hopes, as had been Anna, the mother of Samuel, and likewise Zachary and Elizabeth, the parents of John the Baptist. History relates that Amata was favored with the vision of an Angel, who assured her that the fruit of her womb should be from very infancy the wonder of her people. It is also related that the heavenly messenger also made known to the joyous mother the name, Rita, (signifying right) by which the child was called, to denote her unwonted righteousness in fulfilling the divine law and in cultivating the virtues that adorn the various states of the Christian woman.

Accordingly, from the beginning Rita seemed a child of special Providence, and she plainly manifested the workings of divine grace in her infant soul. Among other marvelous incidents, it is related that at her baptism (1381) four days after her birth, a number of perfectly white bees clustered about the face of the child and between her lips, while parted in an angelic smile, deposited their honey, as a symbol of that sweetness of spirit which should possess this privileged creature in the midst of the world's bitterness.

From her early years the lot of Rita seemed removed from, and raised above, that of other children. Her infant diversions assumed the nature of a continuous practice of virtue, especially of obedience and reverence for her aged parents. The virtue of holy purity she guarded with special vigilance by separating herself from the company of men, while the natural love of her heart was satisfied in holding communion with Jesus, the Spouse of Virgins. Together with interior adornment of soul, Rita was possessed of rare beauty and comeliness, which in turn were greatly enhanced by her native modesty and simplicity of manner. As she advanced in years, she reflected more vividly the inborn beauty of virtue, which nowhere shines forth more resplendently than from the soul of a sinless child.

At the age of twelve years, Rita sought to ratify her mystic espousals with Jesus. Her one desire was to consecrate her virginity to the Lord by the vows of poverty, chastity and obedience, and thus place herself on earth in the ranks of that intrepid army of virgins who are privileged to follow the Lamb whithersoever He goeth in Heaven for eternity.

But here Rita was destined to experience a disappointment in her long and ardently cherished hopes. Her aged parents, for some inexplicable reason wholly at variance with their saintly lives, withheld consent to their daughter's fulfilment of her vocation. Instead, they were intent on seeing her form an alliance of marriage. Accordingly, they favored the suit of a young man, Ferdinand, whose family had attained considerable distinction in the little town of Rocca Porrena on account of its wealth. In the lessons of the Divine Office in honor of Saint Rita, the Church characterizes her suitor and destined husband as a man of morose disposition and sullen habits.

The early biographers of Saint Rita all aver that in foregoing her original purpose of embracing the religious life to enter the bond of wedlock, she was a victim sacrificed to the greed of her parents. To maintain, however, that the child Rita was wholly constrained by parental authority to give her hand in a marriage in which her heart had no part, is truly a grievous blot upon the memory of the venerable Antonio and his wife, as well as irreconcilable with the profound affection in which they held their only child. Aside from reference to the special providence which God exercises over his chosen servants, and to the mysterious ways by which He conducts them to the ultimate goal of sanctity, may we not, without lessening aught of Rita's claim to holiness, exculpate the parents from the guilt of having sacrificed the person and happiness of their child to the greed of wealth and worldly preferment?

In justice to all concerned, it would seem that Rita, as yet comparatively a child under the influence of her parents, and in response to the ardent pleadings of a devoted suitor, was diverted from her original intent of embracing the more perfect state of life and yielded consent to enter marriage, influenced more by the pleadings of the youthful Ferdinand than by the persuasion of her parents. The faults and follies of her impetuous wooer were calculated to appeal powerfully to the self-sacrificing spirit of Rita, who too readily confided in the hope of curbing his fierce nature by her own meekness. Many an unhappy marriage may be traced to that exaggerated confidence which the trust of women have in their ability to reform and to reclaim evildoers, and to their willingness to be sacrificed for the betterment of those whom they love. Too often are found those whose innocence of life, like that of Rita, permits them to know evil only by name. They are deluded by this chimera, because they are most liable to misjudge the depths of human depravity and forget that he who is faithless to his God and his own manhood is seldom stayed from the pursuit of evil, either by the pleadings or the devotion of the noblest of women.

CHAPTER II

The world is no stranger to the sad story in which the memory of the heroic St. Monica is bequeathed to posterity. The sorrows which rent her soul in grief have been the inheritance of innumerable wives and mothers of succeeding generations. Many, too, are the struggling hearts that have been crushed beneath the burden which this holy woman sanctified by her tears and her prayers.

The ever memorable home in distant Africa, whose native cheer and brightness were blighted by the combined wickedness of an erring husband and a wayward son, was vividly portrayed in the unhappy marriage of Rita of Cascia. From bright dreams wherein were indulged fond hopes of reclaiming the prodigal husband, the young wife was soon rudely awakened to a full sense of the appalling sacrifice she had made, in plighting her faith to a spouse whose ardent wooing was in marked contrast with his utter disregard of the duties of a Christian husband. The pagan father of Augustine was not further removed from the maxims of the Gospel than was the worldly and dissipated Ferdinand, into whose keeping the parents of Rita surrendered their only child.

His was a master mind in fostering those bitter strifes and feuds, which waxed strong in his day, and were too often perpetuated with increasing virulence from generation to generation. Frequently was his hand raised in deadly combat, despite the prayers and entreaties of his wife. Upon her and the home she dignified by her virtues he looked with indifference and treated them with woeful neglect, while his heart was allured by the ill-fated delights that are found in debauchery and riot. In this bitter experience, Rita of Cascia was schooled during the early years of her married life. Through it she learned how powerless were her efforts to elicit from her husband that love and affection she so eagerly coveted, or to restrain him in his ruthless career of vice and dissipation. Though the heart of her husband reposes not in her the well-merited trust, yet will she prove herself the valiant woman, "who will render him good, and not evil all the days of his life."

Like a giant figure from out a storm, there rose from Rita's lone grief a calm resolve, that the heavy yoke which bowed her neck shall not be borne in vain. Though the husband of her choice had by his infidelity forfeited that pure love which her heart so generously bestowed upon him at the altar, and thus robbed her of the pearl of earthly happiness, yet will she forget the grievous wrong in the all-consuming desire to win to God that soul which brought anguish to her heart. To this end Rita bends the powers of mind and body, and generously does she consecrate her sufferings and her prayers in the one hope that, as she sows in tears, so may she reap with delight the bounteous harvest in the Lord's own good day.

From the smouldering ruins of a wife's outraged affections bursts the fire of an apostle's zeal. A voice within her soul, whose gentle echo chides the rising emotions of resentment, tells her she is the divinely appointed vessel of election through which the soul of a faithless husband shall be restored to the inheritance of grace which he so dishonored. The consciousness that his ill-requited love has blighted the joy of her young life and clouded her home with the gloom of mingled shame and sorrow, is swallowed up in the burning zeal for the salvation of a soul. For eighteen long years this hope is the one ray of light to relieve the darkness that beset the path of Rita of Cascia, the one abiding comfort to support her jaded spirit, as she goes back in memory to the happy days of her childhood, and realizes how abortive have been the results of her once cherished desires for the quiet and peace of the cloister.

In lieu of this haven of repose, which God reserves for the favored few, poor Rita in a fatal hour elected to embark upon a sea of bitterness, the fury of whose storm she was now struggling heroically to buffet. The lesson of St. Monica, whom she had, early in her career of misfortune, chosen as model and patroness, appeals powerfully to her in the midst of her abandonment and sorrow. The heavy cross she espouses with ready cheerfulness, if only by it she can uplift from sin and shame a reckless, recreant husband. To friends and acquaintances, who could not be ignorant of the notorious misdeeds of Ferdinand and the consequent unhappiness that pervaded her home, Rita deigned no word of complaint. God alone was her comfort; to Him who knew the secrets of her heart, she had refuge in tears and in prayers. When other wives had recourse to her to relate their unhappiness, she was always quick to shield husbands from excessive censure. She was wont to say on such occasions: "Bear in mind that the wife who speaks ill of her husband is not less at fault than is he whose evil ways have given grounds for the accusation."

The violence which this afflicted woman bore to Heaven by her prayers was not in vain. God at length touched the obdurate heart of Ferdinand, and caused him to see the full iniquity of his former ways. Divine grace flooded his soul with light. Its magic power tames the fierce lion and forthwith transforms him into the meek lamb of the Gospel. Rita rejoices to see her repentant husband wholly resolved on consecrating the residue of his years in atoning for his past iniquities. The God whom he had insulted, the wife, the family and the home, upon whom he had brought sorrow and shame, caused him, like another David, to pour out tears of repentance.

But this crown of happiness, which was awarded Rita of Cascia in answer to her eighteen years of anguish, was destined to be interwoven with new thorns of suffering. Short was to be the respite of her repose. Earthly joys, though sanctified by high and holy aims, were not to be the portion of her inheritance. Not yet had she drained the chalice of bitterness; a thorn-strewn path still lay between her and the goal of peace and comfort. God had reserved a strange, hopeless journey for Rita, in order to make more luminous her claim to the title, "Advocate of the

Impossible," with which Catholic devotion has invested her.

Though the grace of forgiveness was freely bestowed upon the repentant husband, there was still due a debt of human reckoning, a temporal punishment, the discharge of which entailed dread consequences upon himself and his family alike. The dagger of an assassin, who had nourished resentment from strifes of former days, cut short the career of the unfortunate Ferdinand in the first fervor of his repentance.

The bereaved widow, in the paroxysm of her grief, pleaded with equal earnestness before the throne of divine mercy for the soul of her husband, as she interceded at the human tribunal of justice, to save the perpetrators of this tragic deed from the full penalty of their crime. But not so with the two orphans of her charge, whose young hearts nurtured a desire of vengeance upon the slayers of their father. The noble example of the mother's forgiveness, her entreaties and prayers, were all powerless to quench their thirst for the blood of him whose dagger thrust had made them orphans. The Vendetta, so long the curse of Southern Europe, aroused the poor widow to a sense of the awful fate which, in pursuance of its behest, might yet befall her desolate home. Too well she knew that the vow of a kinsman, once registered to avenge the blood of a murdered kith, stifles the voice of conscience and causes men to trample upon the most sacred ties of duty and religion. What if the children of her tears, goaded on by revenge and a misguided sense of honor, should one day imbrue their hands in human blood! Oh, that the curse of Cain should be their inheritance, is a thought too terrible to be entertained. Yet, the fire that gleams from their eyes and the frowning look of sullen resolve that overcasts their countenance, is the orphans' only answer to the mother's entreaties for forgiveness. For the moment Rita is made forgetful of all else, save the consuming dread of the horrors which are foreshadowed in the demeanor of her sons. The forebodings of murder transfix the mother's love. In this hour of over-shadowing despair, Rita of Cascia had reached the cross-road in the journey of bitterness, which an all-wise Providence had marked out for her to tread. Here was to be raised the altar where the sacrifice of a mother's heart would be immolated. The cup of human sorrow is filled to the overflow, as she knelt in prayer, and with an anguish of spirit bordering on despair, cried out: "My God! if these children, with which Thou hast blest me in the days of my sorrow shall avenge a father's murder by defiling their own souls with blood, deign to take them to thy own keeping, ere the crime be enacted."

The prayer of the heart-broken widow was heard. Her two sons were snatched from this world of strife: "Taken away lest wickedness should alter their understanding, or deceit beguile their souls." Within the space of one short year Rita, bereft of all the earth can prize, knelt in tears over the graves of her husband and two sons; while in her solitary grief she bowed in submission to the will of Him who hath said: "Revenge to me, I will repay."

CHAPTER III

The good Queen Blanche was wont to say to her much-loved son, whom we today venerate under the title of St. Louis, King of France: "My child, I should infinitely rather see you fall dead at my feet, than that you would ever commit one mortal sin." God was pleased to accept the sacrifice of this holy woman's will and to reward her desire, as with the Patriarch Abraham, without requiring further proof of her unalterable love.

But the desolate widow of Cascia, in giving expression to the same sentiment in reference to her two sons, must like Job redeem the pledge of her loyalty by the utter abandonment of all that the human heart holds dearest. For generously had she immolated upon the altar of divine love the dearest sacrifice of a mother's heart; and God demanded that this should be made a veritable holocaust or whole burnt-offering of her afflicted soul.

Once freed from the manifold cares and duties that engage a wife and mother, Rita with a singleness of purpose labored for her own greater holiness, as the one thing necessary. She, indeed, was the model widow of the Gospel, whose trust was in God, and she continued in prayer and supplication night and day. In that brave heart which sorrow like a winter's blast had benumbed there was experienced a cheery awakening, as if the springtime of renewed hope had at length dawned. Beneath this holy influence quickened to life the long buried ambition so dearly treasured during her childhood years. To the cloister she turns with a fondness that comes only from God, and she yearns to possess it as the one haven of repose where the calm of holy peace may settle upon her wearied spirit, and God may be served with undivided thought. Full well she knew, however, that the condition of widowhood was an almost insuperable obstacle to her admission into any religious community of Sisters, not to speak of the fact that she was already near thirty-five years of age. After weighing the question well in prayer, she resolves with unfaltering trust in God to exert her utmost to attain the object of her desires. The sequel discloses how law and custom wisely sanctioned by human prudence may at times be at variance with the plans of divine Providence.

At the close of the fourteenth century, contemporary with the events here related, a community of Augustinian Nuns resided in the town of Cascia. Rita's early years were consumed in the devout expectation of being one day numbered among these virgins of the Lord. And afterwards when this holy purpose was defeated by an ill-fated marriage, which reduced her to a veritable bondage, the burden of grief that weighed heavily upon her heart was often uplifted by the consolation afforded her in the frequent visits to this sacred retreat. Here was she taught a love for St. Monica and urged by entreaty of the good Sisters to take the mother of their holy founder Augustine, as the patron of intercession and the model of imitation.

Conscious as the poor widow was of the apparent hopelessness of her petition, she repaired to the convent without delay and courageously asked to be admitted to the society of these religious. Rita, however, in spite of her entreaties, was met with a polite but no less forcible refusal. The good Superioress pointed out the barrier placed by the Rule of the Order against her reception. But the widow of Cascia did not on this account despair of ultimately attaining to the fruition of her desires. Disappointed, but not disheartened, she returned to her home, and gave herself unreservedly to prayer and works of penance, in order that the Lord might obtain for her what, humanly speaking, seemed impossible to attain.

"O woman, great is thy faith: be it done to thee as thou wilt," said Jesus to the woman of Canaan who, despite rebuffs, importuned Him the more fervently for the health of her daughter. God wishes us to go to Him with humility and confidence in moments of greatest trial; for we not only thus honor Him, but also learn to value aright the blessings we stand so much in need of. Oftentimes He singles out the objects of His predilection from among those whose positions in life are so obscure and their sufferings so commonplace, as to escape the observation of the world. Thus are we taught that virtue alone lifts man to eminence and distinction in the mind of Him whose eyes are always upon the just and whose ears are attentive to their prayers.

Rita was chosen by God to exemplify in a most striking manner the triumph of an enduring faith and constancy. One night shortly after her disappointing visit to the good Sisters in Cascia, she was suddenly interrupted in her fervent prayers by the sound of a voice of inexpressible sweetness, saying: "Rita, Rita, thy prayers have been received with favor; God grants thee the fruition of thy desires." Astonished at the reality of the sound, she was yet further entranced by the sudden apparition of St. John the Baptist followed immediately by St. Augustine and St. Nicholas of Tolentine, the three special advocates of her devotion. These made known to her that God had been pleased to close the period of her sorrows. At the instance of these heavenly messengers, she forthwith rose from her kneeling posture and following their guidance, repaired direct to the Augustinian convent. Within its portals she was admitted unknown to the community, without loosening bolt or bar. The mysterious guides at once disappeared, leaving Rita kneeling in reverential awe to await the moment when her presence should become known to the community.

The poor widow amidst tears of joy told the astonished Sisters the means by which she had gained access to their cloister. "I beseech you," she exclaimed in finishing this strange recital, "for the sake of the Lord who has shown in my regard His boundless mercy, that you deign to admit me into your society." An interior light, more convincing than the words of Rita, forced upon the whole community the conviction that the operations of the Most High were apparent in her presence among them. Accordingly, she who had been previously rejected as unsuited to their companionship, was now welcomed with sentiments of mingled joy and reverence, as they successively impressed the kiss of peace upon this angel of peace, whom God had so mysteriously sent them.

This marvelous incident attending Saint Rita's entrance to religion was duly examined and authenticated as one of the miracles which the Holy See admitted in the process of her beatification. It is also embodied in the lessons of the Divine Office, which is recited in her honor by the Augustinians on the twenty-second day of May of each year. Occurring as the first miracle recorded in the life of this privileged servant of God, it marks an epoch in her earthly career. It came as a helping hand outstretched from Heaven to uplift a patient, suffering soul from the uttermost depths of adversity. It is a beautiful example of the watchful care that God bestows upon the patient sufferer whom the world despises...... Rita, as the child of St. Augustine, in seeking after perfection through the observance of his holy Rule, became a spectacle to men and angels of those virtues which befit the followers of the Immaculate Lamb. The inborn pride of the human heart she subdued by obedience and humility of an heroic degree; while she not less effectually chastened the bodily senses by the most rigorous penances.

Her special devotion centered upon the mysteries of the cross and upon the sorrows Jesus Christ endured when He was nailed to it for love of man. So consuming was the fire of love awakened within her soul by the contemplation of the sorrows of the Savior that, while prostrate one day at the foot of the crucifix, she besought the Lord to cause her to feel some share of the sufferings which He experienced in His agony on Calvary. Marvelous to relate, a thorn was instantly detached from the crown that encircled the brow of the holy figure before which she was kneeling and, being guided by some unseen hand, imbedded its dart in the forehead of the devout suppliant, causing her intense pain, which together with the wound it inflicted remained with her until death. This singular pledge of the divine love which Jesus bore his devoted client served as the indescribable torment which crystallized the virtues of Saint Rita. It was like a mysterious fountain replenishing with untold delights her spiritual nature during life, and an abiding mark of predestination, that as she patiently suffered, so also should she reign with Jesus.

CHAPTER IV

Saint Rita, in her ardent devotion to the passion of Jesus Christ, verified amidst sufferings the prediction of the Prophet: "You shall draw waters of joy from the fountains of your Savior." The inexhaustible source of comfort to the holy nun in the latter years of her life seemed to have come from her prolonged meditations before the crucifix. From a vivid sense of our Lord's sufferings she was often lifted to the contemplation of the delights of Heaven, repeating in moments of highest ecstasy: "It is not in the power of human language to describe the life of an angel."

At this time (1450) when Rita was grievously afflicted with the mysterious wound upon her forehead, the Sovereign Pontiff proclaimed a jubilee of indulgence to all who visited Rome. Custom in those ages sanctioned the right of religious communities to visit Rome in such special seasons of grace. Rita, however, was threatened with the denial of this privilege on account of the disfigurement of her face, consequent on the wound upon her forehead. At this juncture, in answer to her prayers, she was suddenly relieved of all appearance of the sore, although she remained sensitive to the pain, which never departed from her in this life. But immediately upon her return to the convent after her pilgrimage the mysterious affliction reappeared.

Owing to this unsightly wound upon the forehead of Saint Rita, she was permitted to occupy a portion of the convent secluded from the public and from the remaining members of the community. Here in her solitude she was seldom disturbed, and her constant companions were limited to the snow white bees which had followed her from her home at Rocca Porena to the Augustinian convent. These bees of a singular species took up their abode near the nun's cell, over the door. They to this day live a solitary life; do not mate; and only appear in Holy Week of each year, when, issuing from their cavities, they remain visible until the feast of their Queen, Rita, May 22. Afterward they immediately return to their tiny hermitages in the wall. Each bee inhabits a particular retreat, not like the ordinary bee-comb, but a long narrow hole, as if made by a nail or a thorn. On returning to its wonted seclusion, each bee closes the entrance to its cell with a delicate, white gossamer like web or tissue, and there stays as if in contemplation, during the rest of the year.

These strange companions of Rita are not known to eat or to grow in number or even to die. They possess neither sting nor mandible and never disturb the cloister silence with their hum. They are indeed veritable anchorites. One of this strange collection was enclosed in a crystal vase, and sent by special request to Pope Urban VIII, by whom Rita was beatified, July 16, 1625. The Sovereign Pontiff marveled at the significant character of the bee, which he quaintly called a member of the new Augustinian Order.

The bee, after remaining one day with the Pope, suddenly disappeared. On inquiry it was found snug at home with its associates in Cascia where they have continued undisturbed ever since, to the wonder and astonishment of many.

The foregoing facts, confirmed by reliable witnesses, have been the theme of several beautiful stanzas of poetry.

The last illness of Rita covered a period of four years, during which God permitted her bodily sufferings to serve as the final process for crystallizing her soul and fitting it for the sight of the beatific vision. At these times, when her senses seemed dulled with pain and distress, a gift of superior understanding savoring of the miraculous was vouchsafed her. Once when visited by a lady friend and close relative the sick religious said: "Go, for the love of Jesus, to the garden attached to the home of my parents, and there pluck a rose and bring it to me." It was then the month of January; the ground was frozen; snow and frost abounded; vegetation was paralyzed. The friend obeyed the invalid from a motive merely of gratifying a deluded fancy, but with no thought of finding the promised flower. Great was her surprise, however, on reaching the garden to see a tiny rose peeping through the surrounding snow, possessing the bloom and fragrance of spring. Hastily she returned to the bedside of Rita, and exhibited the rose, to the amazement of all present. On another occasion during the same month, this friend visited the afore-mentioned garden at Rita's request, and brought her two figs found there upon a tree. This tree was pointed out as an object of wonder and reverence by the people of Cascia, as recently as the early portion of the present century. It seemed the Holy Ghost, who had found her soul so agreeable a dwelling-place, now in her last illness deluged it with delights. The marvels of the figs and flowers were the outward evidence of the internal voice of this Divine Spirit speaking to her. "Arise, my love, and come......The winter is now past......The flowers have appeared in our land......The fig-tree hath put forth her green figs;

the vines in flower yield their sweet smell."

The mortal life of this holy nun was prolonged to the following month of May. God, it would seem, delayed her days of suffering in order to edify those who were privileged to surround her in her last illness and to cleanse her soul of every taint of dross. She was forewarned by supernatural power of the approach of death. On awakening from a long stupor, during which the Sisters feared that life was extinct, she spoke with apparent pleasure: "I know that I am going to die, that I shall soon close my eyes to the world to open them only on God."

After receiving the last Sacraments, and bidding farewell to the Sisters and earnestly exhorting them to pray for her soul, a calm and holy quiet possessed her, as one asleep. To the amazement of the nuns, who were kneeling in prayer and tears by her bedside, the pallor of death was suddenly succeeded by the color of health and vigor. Her pale, emaciated features were marvelously transformed to the appearance of a young girl of twenty years. The

Sisters, amazed at the sight of this inexplicable reality, were awed in reverence by the assurance of Saint Rita, on recovering consciousness, that her advocates St. John the Baptist, St. Augustine and St. Nicholas of Tolentine had appeared to her. Then with apparent vigor of body, she addressed the nuns: "Dear Sisters, let God alone occupy your hearts. Observe with exactness the rule which you have professed and venerate our holy Father Augustine, who has laid down in it the royal path to glory."

Such was the last will and testament of this holy woman, which she further accentuated with the exhortation: "My dear ones, abide with the Lord in holy peace and fraternal charity." She closed her eyes again and with the gentleness of slumber breathed her soul to God, May 22, 1457, in the seventy-sixth year of her mortal life.

For many days the body of Saint Rita was exposed to public veneration. The mysterious transformation of her aged and attenuated features to the semblance of youth was apparent to all who viewed the remains. Even to this day the phenomenon may be witnessed. A distinguished ecclesiastic now residing in this country, was privileged recently to examine, in an official capacity, the body of St. Rita. He avers that the body, though cadaverous in appearance, is still in a perfect state of preservation, possessing all the outlines of youth.

CONCLUSION

Blessed Rita was canonized on the 24th of May, 1900. The steps that led up to this culmination were the ones usually taken in such cases though hastened by the zeal and devotion of one who had already given much time and labor to the same object. This was Cardinal Sebastian Martinelli, late Apostolic Delegate to the United States of America and former Prior General of the Augustinian Order. It may not generally be known that the office of Postulator of Causes for Augustinian Saints was at one time filled by His Eminence, then living as a simple priest of his Order in the old convent of Posterula at Rome. From the recent canonization of Blessed Rita, we may infer that nothing was left undone by him to raise to the honors of the altar those holy Augustinians who had died in the odor of sanctity. As General of his Order he found fresh opportunities and means of furthering the object he had so much at heart. During his tenure of this office, a new examination into the causes of the marvelous odor that exhaled continuously from the body of Blessed Rita was permitted by apostolical authority in the year 1892. The examination took place in the presence of Father Martinelli and the Promoter of the Faith, Mgr. Caprara, the result of the process being declared valid by the Sacred Congregation of Rites in 1895. This finding was a confirmation of the conclusion reached by the examiners appointed for the same purpose in the year 1626.

To establish a right to canonization, three miracles must be proved to have taken place, since the person was declared Blessed. There were four of such cases under process of examination, with regard to Blessed Rita, in the hope that three of them, at least, could be established to the satisfaction of the Congregation of Rites. But the Holy Father was content with the three first presented and dispensed with the fourth, the miraculous cure of an Augustinian nun in 1735.

The virtues of Blessed Rita were declared heroic by the Sacred Congregation, with the approbation of His Holiness in 1897. Two years later, a preparatory discussion of the three miracles was begun by the Congregation. On March 27, 1900, the general and final discussion terminated favorably, and the question was proposed to the Holy Father, whether in case the miracles were approved by him, the canonization of Blessed Rita could with safety be undertaken. Having secured the votes of the Cardinals and Consultors on the subject, the Holy Father declared the cause most noble and acceptable, but deferred supreme and final judgment until April 8th, which he then gave forth in two decrees. In the first he declared that the miracles worked through the intercession of Blessed Rita were fully proved—first, as to the wonderful odor emanating from her sacred remains, which diffused itself abroad and effected remarkable cures whenever her intercession was sought; second, the instantaneous cure of Elizabeth Bergamini from inflammation of the eyes; and third, as to the sudden and permanent restoration to health of Cosimus Pellegrini afflicted with chronic catarrh and anaemia. In the second decree he declared that the canonization of Blessed Rita could be safely proceeded with.

From the accounts given in the various decrees setting forth the reasons for thus honoring this holy servant of God and from other historical sources, as well, Saint Rita appears as an extraordinary and illustrious model for every condition of Christian womanhood—maiden, wife, mother, widow, nun. Born on the 22nd of May, she consecrated the first twelve years of her life to holy childhood in domestic retirement; for the next eighteen years of her youth, she endured the assaults of an ill-tempered husband with such sweetness and patience as finally to arouse in him a spirit of repentance and a sense of Christian duty; the two years following his edifying death were passed in devout exercises of religion, when her desire to consecrate herself entirely to God's service was miraculously obtained and within convent walls she passed the remaining forty-four years of her mortal existence, leading the perfect life of a religious, until her beautiful soul winged its glad flight to Heaven.

In the Consistory of April 19th, 1900, the canonization of Blessed Rita was asked for and the Holy Father expressed his great joy at being able to grant the request, but first wished to have the opinion of the Episcopate. The Cardinals and Bishops gave their consent in the Consistory of May 17th, and the Holy Father appointed the 24th of the same month for the ceremony of canonization. Special devotions were proclaimed in preparation for the event, which was at length celebrated with the grandest pomp and splendor amid the joyful acclamations of thousands drawn to the Holy City by their desire to gain the great Jubilee indulgence of that year. The enthusiasm reached its height when the Holy Father, to whom alone pertains the right of proclaiming a Saint, decreed and defined that Blessed Rita of Cascia, professed nun of the Order of Saint Augustine, was a Saint and was hereby inscribed on the catalogue of Saints and that her memory should be held in perpetual veneration on the 22nd of May each year by the Universal Church. In the Name of the Father and of the Son and of the Holy Ghost. Amen.

Thus closes the last act in the life-drama of a true servant of God. And while the canonization of Saint Rita adds nothing to her glory and happiness in Heaven, it emphasizes the virtues she so nobly practised on earth and sets her more clearly before us as a model for imitation. It only remains for us to go forward, courageously determined to conquer the difficulties that beset our pathway through life, bearing ever in mind the fact that the grace by which she overcame the world is also ours.

Saint Rita, pray for us!

Christ Appears to St. Rita

Andachtsübungen zu Ehren der hl. Rita von Cascia.

O hl. Rita, unsere Patronin und Führerin, wir legen diese Gebete und diese Litanei, nebst den Gedanken, Arbeiten und Leiden unseres Lebens dir zu Füßen. Möge unser Leben durch die tägliche Betrachtung deiner Reinheit, Geduld und Heiligkeit ein schwaches Abbild des Deinigen werden, bis wir sicher zur seligen Ewigkeit gelangen.

Litanei zur hl. Rita von Cascia.

Herr, erbarme dich unser!
Christe, erbarme dich unser!
Herr, erbarme dich unser! Christe, höre uns!
Christe, erhöre uns!
Gott Vater, allmächtiger Schöpfer, Erbarme dich unser!
Gott Sohn, Erlöser der Welt, der du gesagt hast: „Bittet, und ihr werdet empfangen, suchet, und ihr werdet finden, klopfet an, und es wird euch aufgetan werden," Erbarme dich unser!
Gott Heiliger Geist, Geist der Weisheit, des Verstandes, des Rates und der Stärke, Erbarme dich unser!

Heilige Dreifaltigkeit, ein einiger Gott, Erbarme dich unser!

Hl. Maria, die du niemanden eine Bitte abschlägst, Bitte für uns!

Unbefleckte Jungfrau, Königin des Himmels und der Erde,

Unsere Liebe Frau vom heiligsten Herzen Jesu,

Heilige Engel, Geister der Demut, Bittet usw.

Ihr heiligen Fürstentümer, Beschützer der religiösen Genossenschaften,

Ihr heiligen Kräfte, Engel des Starkmutes,

Ihr heiligen Cherubim, Engel des Lichtes,

Hl. Rita, du Fürsprecherin der Hoffnungslosen, Bitte für uns!

Hl. Rita, beseelt von Demut,

Hl. Rita, dem lieben Gott geweiht,

Hl. Rita, du Liebhaberin des Gekreuzigten,

Hl. Rita, du Braut des leidenden Heilandes,

Hl. Rita, erfüllt von Mitleid über das Leiden Christi,

Hl. Rita, vom Engel mit einer Dornenkrone gekrönt,

Hl. Rita, die du die Wundmale dieser geheimnisvollen Krönung an deiner Stirne trugst,

Hl. Rita, felsenfest vertrauend auf die milde Barmherzigkeit Jesu,

Hl. Rita, die du mit heißem Flehen den sterbenden Erlöser bestürmst,
Hl. Rita, die du die Erhörung des Gebetes niemals bezweifelt hast,
Daß wir aller Selbstliebe entsagen, Bitte für uns, o hl. Rita!
Daß wir den Verheißungen Christi vertrauen,
Daß die Feinde unseres Heiles zu Schanden gemacht werden,
Daß wir stets den Willen Gottes vollkommen erfüllen,
Daß die Neigung zum Bösen in uns zerstört werde,
Daß der Glaube sich in all seiner Reinheit über unser Land ausbreite,
Daß ein heiliger Eifer unser Herz erfülle,
Daß wir allen, mit denen wir in Berührung kommen, eine heilige Liebe zur Reinheit einflößen,
Daß wir uns stets bei all unserm Tun und Lassen einer zarten Nächstenliebe befleißen,
Daß wir von aller Habgier, Ehrsucht, und allem freventlichen Urteil befreit werden,
Daß große Heilige in unserm Lande erstehen, die das Volk erbauen und die Finsternisse des Unglaubens erhellen,
Daß wir von allen innerlichen Feinden befreit werden,

O du Lamm Gottes, das du hinwegnimmst die Sünden der Welt, Verschone uns, o Herr!
O du Lamm Gottes, das du hinwegnimmst die Sünden der Welt, Erhöre uns, o Herr!
O du Lamm Gottes, das du hinwegnimmst die Sünden der Welt, Erbarme dich unser!

℣. Bitte für uns, o hl. Rita,

℟. Auf daß wir würdig werden der Verheißungen Christi.

Lasset uns beten.

O Gott, der du in deiner unendlichen Barmherzigkeit dich gewürdigt hast, auf das Gebet der hl. Rita zu achten, und ihr zu gewähren, was der menschlichen Einsicht unmöglich scheint, zur Belohnung für ihre Liebe und ihr festes Vertrauen auf deine Verheißungen, habe Mitleid mit unserm Elend, und hilf uns in unserer Trübsal, damit die Ungläubigen erfahren mögen, daß du der Lohn der Demütigen, die Verteidigung der Schwachen, und die Stärke jener bist, die auf dich vertrauen, durch Christum unsern Herrn. Amen.

Gebet zur hl. Rita.

O heilige Beschützerin jener, die sich in der größten Hilflosigkeit befinden, die du glänzest als ein Hoffnungsstern in mitte der Finsternisse, glorreiche hl. Rita, hell leuchtender Spiegel der katholischen Kirche, geduldig und stark wie der Patriarch Job, du Schrecken der bösen Geister, du Stärke der Schwachen, du Helferin in äußerster Not, du Bewunderung der Heiligen, und Vorbild aller Stände; mit ganzem Herzen und mit ganzer Seele, fest vereinigt mit dem anbetungswürdigsten Willen Gottes, durch die Verdienste unseres Herrn und Erlösers Jesu Christi und besonders durch die Verdienste seiner geduldigen Tragung der schmerzlichen Dornenkrone, die du täglich mit der größten Andacht betrachtetest, durch die Verdienste der allerseligsten Jungfrau Maria und deiner eigenen erhabenen Tugenden bitten wir inständigst, uns die Gewährung unseres Anliegens zu erflehen. (Hier trage dein Anliegen vor.) O huldvolle Beschützerin und Fürsprecherin, leite uns und läutere unsere Meinungen, damit wir die Verzeihung unserer Sünden erlangen und die Gnade, wie du, täglich mit Mut, Opferwilligkeit und unwandelbarer Treue jenen Weg zum Himmel zu wandeln, den die Liebe unseres Herrn uns führen will. Amen.

Hl. Rita, Fürsprecherin der Hoffnungslosen, bitte für uns!

Hl. Rita, Sachwalterin des Unmöglichen, bitte für uns!

(Drei Vater unser, Gegrüßet seist du, Maria, Ehre sei dem Vater.)

Gebenedeit sei Gott, der Vater unseres Herrn Jesu Christi, Vater der Barmherzigkeit und Gott alles Trostes, der uns durch die Fürsprache der hl. Rita in all unseren Trübsalen trösten wolle. Amen.

O glorreiche hl. Rita, die du wunderbarer Weise an dem bitteren Leiden unseres Herrn Jesu Christi Anteil nahmst, erlange uns die Gnade, mit Ergebung die Widerwärtigkeiten dieses Lebens zu ertragen, und beschütze uns in all unsern Nöten. Amen.

(300 Tage Ablaß einmal täglich.)

Gebet.

Mächtige Patronin jener, die sich in Not befinden, hl. Rita, so demütig, keusch und geduldig, du, deren inständigen Bitten dein göttlicher Bräutigam nicht widerstehen kann, erflehe für uns von deinem gekreuzigten Jesus Gewährung unserer Bitte. Sei uns gewogen und erhöre uns gnädigst zur größeren Ehre Gottes und zu deinem Ruhme, und wir versprechen, dich stets zu ehren und fernerhin dein Lob zu singen. Amen.

Gebet zur hl. Rita.

O glorreiche hl. Rita, vollkommene Jüngerin des sanftmütigen und geduldigen Jesus von Nazareth, um deiner tiefen Demut willen, mit welcher du die niedrigsten Dienste im Kloster zu Cascia ausübtest, nachdem dein heiliger Beschützer dich in dasselbe durch verschlossene Türen eingeführt hatte, wo du ein in Christo verborgenes Leben führtest nach der Regel des hl. Augustinus, wir bitten dich, erflehe für uns von Gott, der dem Hoffärtigen widersteht und dem Demütigen seine Gaben verleiht, die Gnade, der Hoffart zu widerstehen, dieser Hauptquelle all unseres Elendes, damit wir würdig werden, dereinst wie unser göttlicher Erlöser zur ewigen Glorie zu erstehen.

Ihm zur Ehre lasset uns beten: Vater unser, Gegrüßet seist du, Maria, Ehre sei dem Vater.

Die Fürbitterin der Hoffnungslosen, die hl. Rita, wurde am 24. Mai 1900 heilig gesprochen. Sie ist allgemein bekannt als „Die Heilige des Unmöglichen," da ihre Fürbitte sich in den hoffnungslosesten Fällen bewährt hat.

℣. Du hast deine Dienerin Rita bezeichnet

℟. Mit den Zeichen deiner Liebe und deiner Leiden.

Lasset uns beten.

O Gott, der du der hl. Rita wegen ihrer Feindesliebe die Gnade verliehen hast, in ihrem Herzen und an ihrer Stirne die Merkmale deiner Liebe und deiner Leiden zu tragen, verleihe uns, wir bitten dich, daß wir durch ihre Fürbitte und um ihrer Verdienste willen von den Dornen wahrer Reue durchdrungen werden und fortwährend deiner Leiden gedenken, der du lebst und regierst von Ewigkeit zu Ewigkeit. Amen.

(Drei Vater unser, Gegrüßet seist du, Maria, Ehre sei dem Vater.)

NEUVAINE EN L'HONNEUR DE STE. RITA.

O bienheureuse Ste. Rita, notre patronne et notre avocate, nous déposons cette couronne à vos pieds, comme nous le faisons de nos pensées, de nos travaux, de nos souffrances, afin qu'animés par vos exemples de pureté, de patience et de sainteté, nos vies puissent être conformes à la vôtre dans la béatitude éternelle.

LITANIES DE STE. RITA DE CASCIA.

Seigneur, ayez pitié de nous.
Christ, ayez pitié de nous.
Seigneur, ayez pitié de nous.
Christ, écoutez nous.
Christ, exaucez nous.
Dieu le Père Tout Puissant, ayez pitié de nous.
Dieu le Fils, Rédempteur du monde qui avez dit: "Demandez et vous recevrez cherchez et vous trouverez frappez et il vous sera ouvert," ayez pitié de nous.

Dieu le St. Esprit, Esprit de Sagesse, d'Intelligence, de Conseil et de Science ayez pitié de nous.

Ste. Marie, qui n'avez jamais refusé ceux qui vous ont invoquée, priez pour nous.

Marie Immaculée, Reine du ciel et de la terre, priez pour nous.

Notre Dame du Sacré Coeur,

Saints Anges, Esprits d'humilité,

Principautés, protectrices des communautés religieuses,

Vertus, anges d'énergie,

Chérubins, anges de lumière,

Ste. Rita, avocate des causes désesperées,

Ste. Rita, éprise de l'humilité,

Ste. Rita, consacrée à Dieu,

Ste. Rita, amante de Jésus crucifié,

Ste. Rita, épouse de Jésus souffrant,

Ste. Rita, pénétrée de compassion pour Notre Seigneur,

Ste. Rita, couronnée par un ange de la sainte couronne d'epines,

Ste. Rita, qui avez porté sur votre front les stigmates de ce couronnement surnaturel,

Ste. Rita, confiante en la tendre miséricorde de Jésus,

Ste. Rita, suppliant avec une ferveur irrésistible Notre Seigneur mourant,
Ste. Rita, ne doutant jamais d'étre exaucée,
Que nous renoncions a tout respect humain,
Que notre confiance soit dans les promesses du Christ,
Que les ennemis de notre salut soient mis en fuite,
Que nous accomplissions parfaitement la sainte volonté de Dieu,
Que nous soyons délivrés de la puissance des ténèbres
Que la foi se répande dans l'univers entier,
Qu'un saint zèle embrase nos coeurs,
Que nous soyons des émulateurs de la pureté,
Que la charité soit le mobile de nos actions,
Que nous nous gardions de toute avarice, de vaine gloire et de jugement téméraire,
Que des grands saints surgissent de notre nation pour édifier le peuple et . dissiper les ténèbres de l'infidélité,
Que nous soyons délivrés de tout ennemi intérieur

Agneau de Dieu, qui effacez les péchés du monde, pardonnez nous Seigneur.
Agneau de Dieu, qui effacez les péchés du monde, exaucez nous Seigneur.
Agneau de Dieu, qui effacez les péchés du monde, ayez pítié de nous.

℣. Priez pour nous, Ste. Rita,

℟. Afin que nous soyons dignes des promesses de Jésus Christ.

PRIONS.

O Dieu, qui dans votre infinie bonté avez daigné exaucer les prières de votre servante, Ste. Rita, et qui accordez par son intercession ce qui semble impossible à la prévoyance humaine, en récompense de son amour compatissant et de son ferme espoir en vos promesses, ayez pitié de nos misères, secourez-nous dans nos calamités, afin que l'incrédule sache que vous êtes la récompense des humbles, le défenseur des faibles, la force de ceux qui se confient en vous, par Jésus Christ, Notre Seigneur.

Ainsi soit-il.

PRIÈRE À STE. RITA.

O sainte protectrice de ceux qui sont dans le plus pressant besoin, qui brillez comme une étoile d'espérance au milieu des ténèbres, glorieuse et bienheureuse Ste. Rita, modèle de patience et de force, terreur des démons, santé des malades, secours des infortunés, admiration des saints, patronne de tous les états, prosternés devant vous, unis de coeur et d'âme à l'adorable volonté de Dieu, par les mérites de Notre Seigneur Jésus Christ, et en particulier par ceux acquis dans son couronnement d'épines, par les mérites de la très douce Vierge Marie, par vos vertus et votre puissance, je vous supplie de m'obtenir cette importante grâce, pourvu qu'elle soit conforme à la plus grande gloire de Dieu et à ma propre sanctification. (ici mentionnez votre demande.) Guidez, purifiez mon intention, ô ma sainte protectrice et ma patronne, afin que je fuisse obtenir le pardon de mes péchés et la grâce de la persévérance quotidienne; qu'à votre exemple je marche avec courage et générosité vers la céleste patrie, où l'amour de mon doux Sauveur me convie.

Ainsi soit-il.

INVOCATIONS À STE. RITA.

Ste. Rita, avocate des désespérés. priez pour nous.

Ste. Rita, avocate des causes impossibles, priez pour nous.

Trois Notre Père, Je vous salue Marie, Gloire soit au Père.

Béni soit Dieu, Père de Notre Seigneur Jésus Christ, Père de miséricorde et Dieu de toute consolation, qui par l'intercession de Ste. Rita nous récomforte dans toutes nos tribulations.

Ainsi soit-il.

O glorieuse Ste. Rita, qui avez miraculeusement participé à la douloureuse Passion de Notre Seigneur Jésus Christ, obtenez-nous de souffrir avec résignation les misères de cette vie, et protégez nous dans tous nos besoins.

PRIÈRE.

Patronne des nécessiteux, Ste. Rita, si humble, pure et patiente, puissante sur le coeur de votre Divin Epoux, obtenez-nous notre demande de Jésus crucifié, Soyez-nous propice pour la plus grande gloire de Dieu et la vôtre; nous vous promettons d'honorer et de chanter vos louanges à jamais.

Ainsi soit-il.

PRIÈRE À STE. RITA.

O glorieuse Ste. Rita, disciple fidèle de l'humble et doux Nazaréen, à cause de cette profonde humilité, pratiquée au milieu des plus humbles devoirs du monastère, où miraculeusement introduite dans le cloître béni de Caseia par votre saint protecteur, vivant de la règle de St. Augustin, vous avez mené une vie cachée en Dieu, nous vous supplions, obtenez-nous de Dieu ennemi des superbes vaincre notre orgueil, cette pernicieuse et soutien des humbles, la grâce de racine de tous nos malheurs afin que nous devenions dignes de parvenir à la gloire éternelle du ciel, à l'exemple de notre divin Rédempteur que nous honorons en disant:.

Notre Père, etc.—Je vous salue Marie, etc.—Gloire soit au Père, etc.

Ste. Rita, avocate des désespérés, fut canonisée le 24 mai 1900. Elle est appellée, "La sainte des choses impossibles," ayant exercé sa puissance dans des causes désesperées.

℣. Vous avez signé votre servante, Rita.

℟. Du signé de votre amour et de votre passion.

PRIONS.

O Dieu qui avez daigné accorder à Ste. Rita, à cause de son amour pour ses ennemis, la faveur de porter dans son coeur et sur son front les stigmates de votre passion, accordez-nous, nous vous en supplions, par son intercession et ses mérites la contrition de nos péchés et la grâce de contempler a jamais les souffrances de votre passion, vous qui vevez et régnez dans les siècles des siècles.

Ainsi soit-il.

Août 11, 1006. Indulgence de 300 jours accordée à tous ceux qui une fois le jour réciteront dévotement la prière suivante en l'honneur de Ste. Rita de Cascia.

SANTA RITA, PREGATE PER NOI.

Devozioni ogni Giovedì, alle ore 9 ant., 2 e 4.30 pom., 7.55 e 8.15 pom.

Oh, Santa Rita Benedetta, nostra patrona e guida, ai tuoi piedi noi deponiamo questa litania, assieme ai nostri pensieri, alle fatiche, alle sofferenze delle nostre esistenze, facendo voti che tenendo continuamente tutt'i giorni dinanzi ai nostri occhi la pazienza e la santità dell esempio che ci avete dato, noi possiamo trascorrere la nostra vita come misero specchio della vita vostra, e ciò perfino nella vita eterna.

LITANIA DI SANTA RITA DA CASCIA.

O Signore, abbi pietà di noi,
Gesù Cristo, abbi pietà di noi.
O Signore, abbi pietà di noi.
Gesù Cristo, ascoltateci.
Gesù Cristo, fateci la grazia d'ascoltarci.
Dio, Padre Onnipotente, abbiate di noi pietà.

Dio, il Figlio, Redentore del mondo che diceste: "Chiedete, e riceverte; cercate, e troverete; bussate, e vi sarà aperto," abbiate pietà di noi.
Dio, lo Spirito Santo, Spirito di Saggezza, di Sapere di Consiglio e di Cognizione, abbiate pietà di noi.
Santa Trinita; un Dio, Potenza Infinita, abbiate pietà di noi.
Santa Maria, che non avete giammai respinto coloro che da voi hanno implorato, pregate per noi.
Maria Immacolata, Regina del Cielo e della Terra, pregate per noi.
Nostra Signora del Sacro Cuore,
Santi Angeli, spiriti di umiltà,
Santi Principi del Cielo, a cui è affidata la cura della comunità religiose,
Sante Virtù, angeli d'energia,
Santi Cherubini, angeli della luce,
Santa Rita, avvocata dell'impossibile
Santa Rita, innamorata dell'umiltà,
Santa Rita, consacrata a Dio,
Santa Rita, amante di Gesù crocifisso,
Santa Rita, sposa di Gesù sofferente,
Santa Rita, penetrata di compassione per il nostro Signore,
Santa Rita, incoronata da un angelo con la sacra Corona di Spine,

Santa Rita, che sopportasti la ferita di questa soprannaturale incoronazione sulla tua fronte,
Santa Rita, che avete sempre fede nella tenera pietà di Gesù,
Santa Rita, che importunate il nostro morente signore con irresistibile fervore,
Santa Rita, che mai dubitateche venga esaudita la preghiera,
Che rinunciamo ad ogni amore verso noi stessi, pregate per noi, Santa Rita.
Che abbiamo fede nelle premesse di Cristo, pregate per noi, Santa Rita.
Che i nemici della nostra salvezza siano confusi,
Che adampiamo più perfettamente la santa volontà di Dio,
Che il potere del male su di noi sia distrutto,
Che la fede possa spandersi in tutta la sua purità per tutta la nostra terra,
Che un santo zelo possa impossessarsi dei nostri cuori,
Che possiamo riuscire a infondere in tutti coloro coi quali noi trattiamo l'amore per la santa purità,
Che possiamo coltivare una delicata carità in tutte le nostre azioni,

Che possiamo essere liberati da ogni avarizia, vanagloria, o da affrettato giudizio,
Che nella nostra nazione sorgano dei grandi santi ad edificare il popolo e ad illuminare le tenebre della mancanza di fede,
Che possiamo essere liberati da tutt'i nemici interni,
Agnello di Dio, che toglieste i peccati del mondo, liberateci, O Signore!
Agnello di Dio, che toglieste i peccati del mondo, fateci la gràzia d'ascoltarci!
Agnello di Dio, che toglieste i peccati del mondo, abbiate pietà di noi, O Signore!
Pregate per noi, Santa Rita,
Che noi veniamo fatti degni delle promesse di Cristo.

PREGHIAMO.

O Dio, che nella Tua infinita misericordia, Ti sei degnato di esaudire la preghiera della Tua serva, Benedetta Rita, e che concedi alle di lei supplicazioni tutto ciò ch'è perfino impossibile al potere umano di compiere, pia come preveggenza, che come abilità e sforzi, a premiare il di lei amore compassionevole e la di lei fede irremovibile nelle Tue promesse; abbi pietà per le nostre avversità e soccorrici nelle nostre calamità, e concedici che i ciechi di fede possano apprendere che Tu sei la ricompensa dell'umile, la difesa dei derelitti, e la forza di coloro i quali hanno fede in Te. Per mezzo di Gesù Cristo. nostro Signore. Così Sia.

PREGHIERA A SANTA RITA.

O santa protettrice di coloro i quali sono in forte bisogno, che risplendi come la stella della speranza tra le tenebre, gloriosa e benedetta Santa Rita, specchio lucente della Chiesa Cattolica, per pazienza e forza come il patriarca Giobbe, peste dei diavoli, salute degli ammalati, liberatrice di quelli che si trovano in estremo bisogno, ammirazione dei Santi e modello di tutti; con tutto il mio cuore e l'anima mia postrato a te dinanzi, e fermamente unito all'adorabile volontà del Signor mio, per i meriti del mio unico Dio e Salvatore, Gesù Cristo, ed in particolare per i meriti della di Lui pazienza nel sopportare le torture di quella corona di spine, che tu, con tenera devozione contemplasti ogni giorno; per i meriti della dolcissima Vergine Maria e della tue stesse eccellenti grazie e virtù, io t'imploro di ottenere che venga a me concessa ciò che fervidamente chiedo—purchè ciò avvenga per la maggior gloria di Dio e per la mia propria santificazione (qui menzionate ciò che chiedete), e qui dentro guidi e purifichi la mia intenzione, O santa Protettrice e carissima Avvocata, onde lo possa ottenere il perdono di tutt'i miei peccati e la grazia di perseverare ogni giorno, come facesti tu, di procedere con coraggio e generosità, e con ferma fede lungo il cammino che porta al Paradiso e in cui l'amore del mio dolce Signore desidera di condurmi. Così Sia.

INVOCATIONI A SANTA RITA.

Santa Rita, Avvocata dei Perduti, prega per noi.

Santa Rita, Avvocata dell'Impossibile, prega per noi.

Tre Pater Noster, Ave Maria, Gloria Patri, ecc.

Sia Benedetto Dio, Padre del Nostro Signore Gesù Cristo, Padre di Misericordia e Dio di tutta la Consolazione, che per mezzo della intercessione di Santa Rita, ci conforta in tutte le nostre tribolazioni. Così Sia.

---

11 Agosto 1006.—Concede un'indulgenza di 300 giorno a tutti coloro i quali una volta al giorno devotamente recitano la seguente preghiera in onore di Santa Rita da Cascia.

Oh, gloriosa Santa Rita, che partecipasti miracolosamente nella dolorosa Passione del Nostro Signore Gesù Cristo, ottieni per me la grazia di soffrire con rassegnazione i triboli di questa vita, e proteggimi in tutt'i miei bisogni.

PREGHIERA.

Santa Patrona di coloro che si trovano in bisogno, santa Rita, così umile, pura e paziente, le cui supplicazioni al vostro Divino Sposo sono irresistibili ottieni per noi la nostra domanda dal tuo crocifisso Gesù. Sii propizia verso di noi per magior gloria di Dio e di te stessa, e noi promettiamo di onorare e di decantare le tuo lodi per sempre. Così Sia.

PREGHIERA A SANTA RITA.

Oh, gloriosa Santa Rita, perfetta discepola del povero ed umile Nazareno, a cagione di quella più che prefonda umiltà che tu esercitasti in mezzo ai piu bassi doveri del convento, dopo che fosti introdotta dal Santo Protettore nel Sacro Chiostro di Cascia attraverso le porte chiuse, e quivi seguendo la Regola di Sant'Agostino tu conducesti una vita nascosta con Cristo in Dio, noi preghiamo te di ottenere per noi da Dio che resiste contro la superbia ed impartisce i Suoi doni agli umili, la grazia di conquidere la passione dell'orgoglio dentro di noi stessi, quella nociva radice di tutt'i nostri guai, onde noi possiamo addivenire degni di essere elevati fino all'eterna gloria del Paradiso, ad imitazione del Nostro Divino Redentore, mentre noi Lo onoriamo dicendo:

Padre Nostro, Ave Maria, Gloria Patri, ecc.

L'AVVOCATA DEI PERDUTI.

Santa Rita fu canonizzata il 24 Maggio 1900. Essa è universalmente chiamata "La Santa della Cose Impossibili," per il fatto che la sua intercessione è stata trovata efficace nei casi più disperati.

NABOŻEŃSTWO DO ŚW. RYTY Z KASCYI.

O błogosławiona św. Ryto, patronok i przewodniczko nasza, składamy u stóp Twoich tę litanią, jako również nasze myśli, prace i cierpienia życiowe; a mając przed oczyma Twoją skromność, czystość, cierpliwość i świątobliwość, chcemy choć w części Ciebie naśladować, aby stać się godnymi żyć z Tobą wiecznie.

LITANIA DO ŚW. RYTY Z KASCYI.

Panie, zmiłuj się nad nami.
Chryste, zmiłuj się nad nami.
Panie, zmiłuj się nad nami.
Chryste, usłysz nas.
Chryste, wysłuchaj nas.
Boże Ojcze Wszechmogący, — Zmiłuj się nad nami.
Boże, Synu Odkupicielu świata, któryś rzekł: proś, a otrzymasz; szukaj a znajdziesz; pukaj, a otworzą ci, Zmiłuj się nad nami.
Boże, Duchu Świety, Duchu Mądrości, Zrozumienia, Rady i Wiedzy, zmiłuj sie nad nami.

Św. Trójco, jedyny Boże, Moco Nieskończona, zmiłuj się nad nami.

Św. Maryo, która nigdy nie opuszczasz tych, którzy Ciebie wzywają, módl się za nami.

Matko Niepokalana, poczęcie, Królowo Nieba i ziemi,

Serce Najświętszej Panny Maryi,

Święci Anieli, duchowie pokory,

Święte Księztwa, opiekunowie zgromadzeń religijnych,

Swiete Moce, aniołowie energii,

Święci Cherubini, anieli światła,

Św. Ryto, pośredniczko nieszczęśliwych,

Św. Ryto, miłośniczko pokory,

Św. Ryto, poświęcona Bogu,

Św. Ryto, wielbicielko Jezusa ukrzyżowanego,

Św. Ryto, oblubienico cierpiącego Jezusa,

Św. Ryto, przepełniona miłością Jezusa,

Św. Ryto, ukoronowana przez anioła koroną cierniową,

Św. Ryto, któraś nosiła na czole rany tej przedziwnej koronacyi,

Św. Ryto, która zaufałaś ze skruchą Jezusowi,

Św. Ryto, któraś okazała umierającemu Jezusowi swoją gorliwość,

Św. Ryto, któraś nigdy nie wątpiła w wysłuchanie Twych modłów,
Abyśmy się mogli pozbyć samolubstwa,
Abyśmy mogli wierzyć w obietnice Chrystusa,
Aby nieprzyaciele naszego zbawienia nie tryumfowali,
Abyśmy mogli wykonać świętą wolę Bożą,
Aby siła złego była unicestwiona,
Aby wiara w całej swej czystości szerzyła się w naszym kraju,
Aby święta gorliwość zawładnęła naszemi sercami,
Abyśmy byli przykładem miłości i świętą czystości dla wszystkich, z kim obcujemy,
Abyśmy w każdym naszym czynie okazywali miłosierdzie,
Abyśmy unikali skąpstwa, pychy i posądzań bliźniego,
Aby wielki święty wyłonił się z naszego narodu, ku zbudowaniu i oświeceniu ciemności i niewiary,
Abyśmy ustrzegli wszystkich wewnętrznych nieprzyjaciół,
Baranku Boży, któryś cierpiał za grzechy świata, Wysłuchaj nas Panie.
Baranku Boży, któryś cierpiał za grzechy świata, Zachowaj nas Panie.

Baranku Boży, któryś cierpiał za grzechy świata, Zmiłuj się nad nami.
Św. Ryto, módl się za nami, Abyśmy się stali godnymi obietnic Chrystusa Pana.

MÓDLMY SIĘ.

O Boże, który w swej nieprzebranej dobroci, obiecałeś wysłuchać modły Twej sługi Błogosławionej Ryty, i wysłuchać Jej orędownictwa, nawet w rzeczach niepodobnych dla ludzkich zdolności i usiłowań, jako nagrodę za Jej miłość i silną wiarę w obietnice Twoje; miej litość nad naszemi ułomnościami i wzmacniaj nas w nieszczęsciach, aby niewierni poznali Twą moc, Twą sprawiedliwość, z jaką nagradzasz pokornych i w Ciebie wierzących, jak wspierasz słabych i pocieszasz zasmuconych.

Przez Pana naszego, Jesuza Chrystusa. AMEN.

MODLITWA DO ŚW. RYTY.

O święta opiekunko potrzebujących, która świecisz jako gwiazda nadziei w ciemnościach, chwalebna i błogosławiona Sw. Ryto, zwierciadło Kościoła Katolickiego, w cierpliwości i meztwie podobna do patryarchy Joba, biczu złych duchow, zdrówie chorych, wybawicielko i wsparcie potrzebujących, podziwie dla Swiętych i wzorze dla osób każdego stanu; całem mojem sercem i dusza scielę sie u stóp Tronu Bożego i mocno sie łaczę ze swiętą Jego wolą, przez zasługi jedynego mego Pana i Zbawiciela Jezusa Chrystusa, a szczególniej przez zasługi Jego cierpliwego noszenia tej boleśnej korony cierniowej, o której ty codziennie rozmysłałas; przez zasługi najsłodszej Panny Maryi i przez twoje wlasne wzniosłe dary i cnoty, błagam cię, przyczyń się do wysłuchania mej usilnej prośby, — aby się tylko ona przyczynić mogła do wiekszej chwały Bożej i mojego uświątobliwienia (tu wymień twoją prośbę) kieruj i strzeż czystości mojej intencyi.

O święta Opiekunko i najdroższa Orędowniczko, wstaw się za mną, abym uzyskał odpuszczenie moich grzechów i łaskę do wytrwania, za twoim przykładem, z odwagą i poświęceniem na drodze do nieba, gdzie milość najdroższęgo Jezusą pragnie mnie prowadzić. AMEN.

BŁAGANIE ŚW. RYTY.

Św. Ryto, Orędowniczko Beznadziejnych, módl się za nami.

Św. Ryto, Orędowniczko w rzeczach Niepodobnych, módl się za nami.

Trzy Ojcze nasz, Zdrowaś Marya, Chwała Ojcu i t. d.

Błogosławiony niech będzie Bóg, Ojciec Pana naszego Jezusa Chrystusa, Ojciec miłosierdzia i Bog wszelmnego pocieszenia, który za wstawienictwem Św. Ryty, osładza nasze cierpienia. AMEN.

O pełna chwały Św. Ryto, która cudownie przejęłaś się bolesną Męką Jezusa Chrystusa, uproś dla mnie łaskę do znoszenia z rezygnacyą moich cierpień życiowych, i strzeż mnie od wszelkich nieszczęść, jakie mają mnie we wszystkich moich potrzebach. AMEN.

Sierpnia 11, 1906 r. Kościół Św. nadał 300 dni odpustu każdemu kto choć raz na dzień odmowi następującą modlitwę do Św. Ryty z Kascyi.

MODLITWA.

Św. Patronko będących w potrzebie; Św. Ryto, tak pokorna, czysta i cierpliwa, której prośby do Bożego Oblubieńca bywają wysłuchane, uzyskaj dla nas od twego ukrzyżowanego Jezusa to, o co Go błagamy. Bądź nam łaskawą dla większej chwały Bożej i twej własnej, a my ci przyrzekamy czcić cię i wielbić po wszystkie czasy. AMEN.

MODLITWA DO ŚW. RYTY.

O pełna chwały, Św. Ryto, doskonała uczenico cichego i pokornego Nazareńczyka, przez twą głęboką pokorę z jaką wykonywałas najniższe usługi w klasztorze w Kascyi, gdzie żyłaś podług reguły Sw. Augustyna, zamknięta z Chrystusem w Bogu, błagamy cię uzyskaj dla nas dar pokory, i łaskę przezwyciężenią pychy, tego szkodliwego zródła wszelkich naszych nieszcześć, abyśmy się stali godnymi Krolestwa Niebieskiego, nasladujac naszego Zdawiciela, którego chwalimy mówiąc:

Ojcze nasz, Zdrowas Maryo, Chwala Ojcu, i t. d.

ORĘDOWNICZKO BEZNADZIEJNYCH.

Św. Ryta była kanonizowaną 24 Maja 1900 roku. Jest powszechnie nazywana „Patronką rzeczy niemożliwych", gdyż jei wstawienictwo było skuteczne w najbardziej rozpaczliwych wypadkach.

INDEX

Emily's Adventures
in Wonderland

Ryan & Julia

CPSIA information can be obtained
at www.ICGtesting.com
Printed in the USA
BVHW042359310119
539208BV00003B/567/P